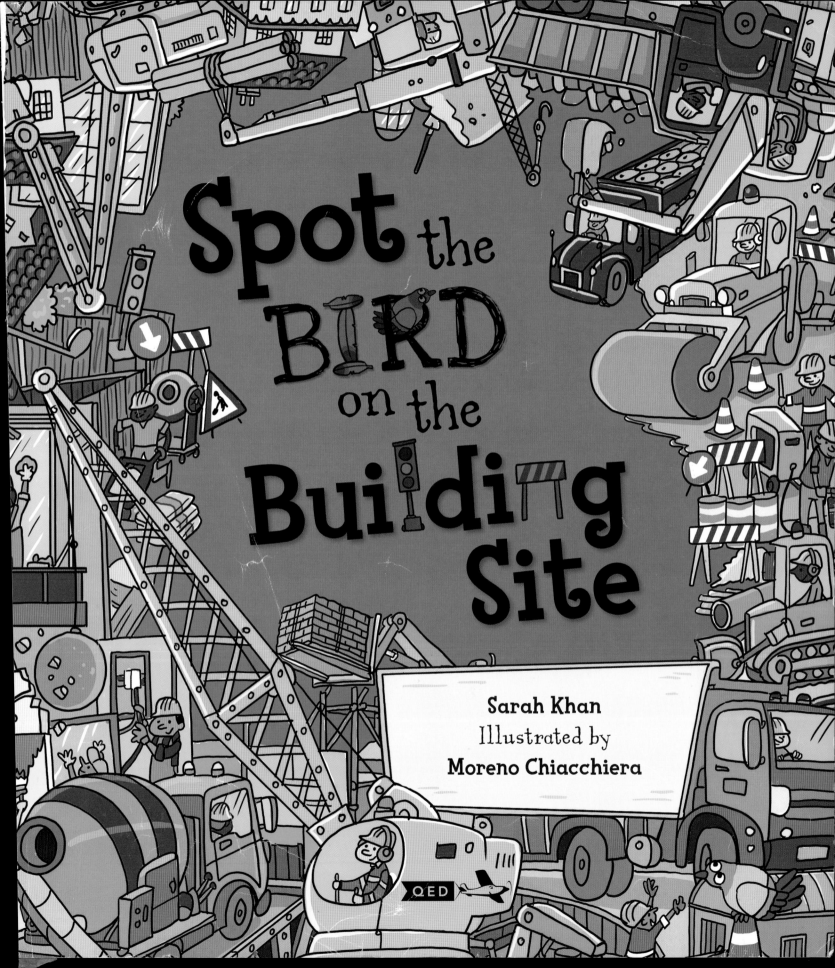

Spot the BIRD on the Building Site

Sarah Khan

Illustrated by
Moreno Chiacchiera

QED

WELCOME TO THE BUILDING SITE!

There's lots to see.
Come and have a look!

Cranes

Building a bridge

Laying a road

Building a house

Laying foundations

Demolition site

Diggers

Playground

Theme park

This bird is hiding inside the book.
Can you find him in every scene?

Can you spot these things?

chair

spirit level

hook

flask

wire cutters

Can you spot these things?

shower head | screwdriver | pink helmet | cement trowel | hammer

A road is made by laying down different layers of sand, stone and concrete, then pressing it all down with a heavy roller.

Can you spot these things?

blue power drill   kayak   plans   buoy   plane

Can you spot these things?

wheelbarrow

paint brush

train

tool box

bucket

Old buildings can be knocked down by wrecking balls and diggers, or blown up using explosives.

The world's tallest crane is also the strongest. It can lift a load the weight of 12 blue whales over 50 storeys high.

Can you spot these things?

spanner

road sign

pick axe

kitchen sink

lunch box

Can you spot these things?

shovel   safety goggles   swing seat   chainsaw   step ladder

More to spot

Go back and find these scenes in the book!

Did you find me?

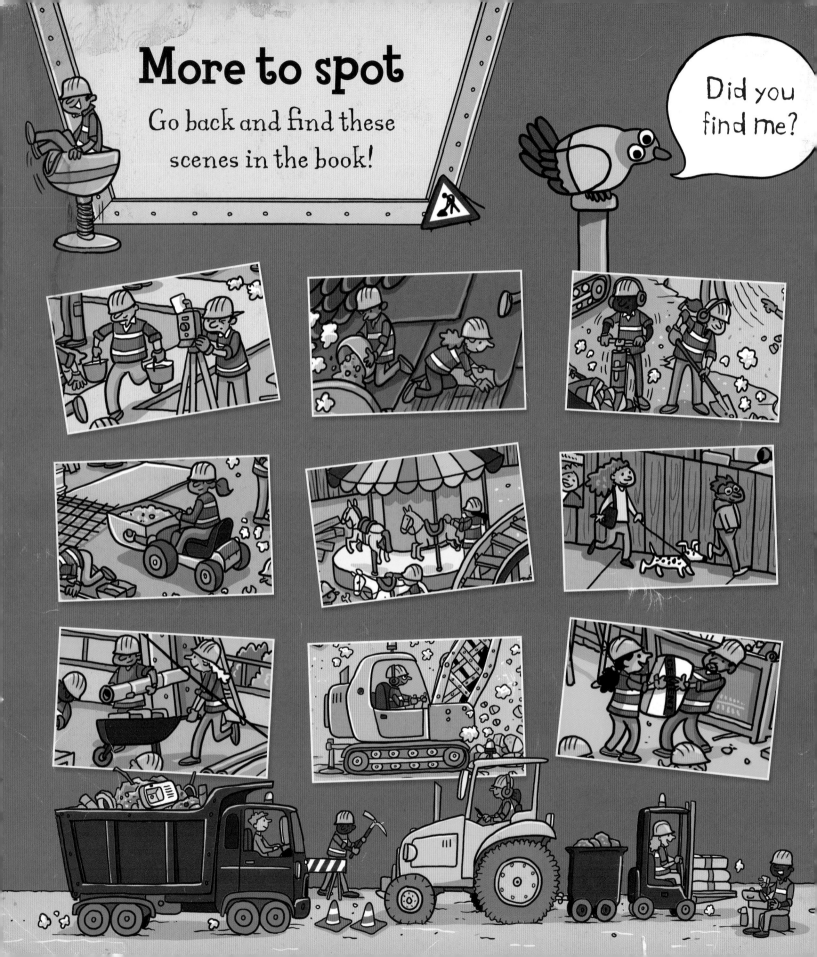

Did you Know?

It takes just 15 seconds for a 30-storey building to be demolished using explosives.

The Shard in London, UK, is over 300 metres tall and has 95 storeys. The average lift speed is 6 metres per second so you can get to the top in less than a minute!

The Chrysler Building, a 77-floor skyscraper in New York, USA, was built very quickly. Four floors were completed every week.

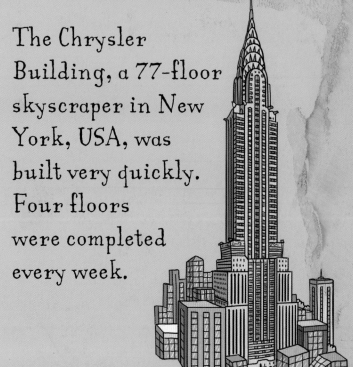

The Ancient Greeks invented cranes over 2000 years ago to help them build temples.

More building fun!

Tissue box bulldozer

Take an empty tissue box and paint large wheels along the sides like a bulldozer. Then ask an adult to cut a cardboard tube lengthways and glue half of it to the front of the box to make the scoop. Put your favourite toy in the hole at the top to drive the bulldozer!

Local building site

If there is a building site near you, try to see what vehicles are on the site next time you walk past. What do you think is being built there?

Make a hard hat

You will need a disposable bowl and a large paper plate. Ask an adult to cut out the middle of the plate to create a rim. Place the rim over the upside down bowl and fix with tape or ask an adult to staple it. Then paint the outside yellow!

Tallest tower

Have a building competition with your friends or family. See who can make the tallest tower out of building blocks or use household objects of different shapes and sizes, such as tin cans or cereal boxes.

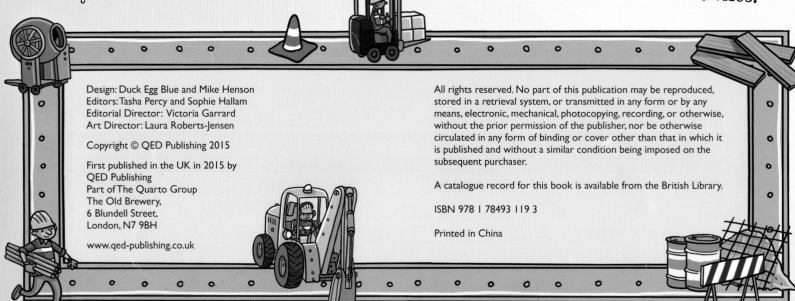

Design: Duck Egg Blue and Mike Henson
Editors: Tasha Percy and Sophie Hallam
Editorial Director: Victoria Garrard
Art Director: Laura Roberts-Jensen

Copyright © QED Publishing 2015

First published in the UK in 2015 by
QED Publishing
Part of The Quarto Group
The Old Brewery,
6 Blundell Street,
London, N7 9BH

www.qed-publishing.co.uk

A catalogue record for this book is available from the British Library.

ISBN 978 1 78493 119 3

Printed in China